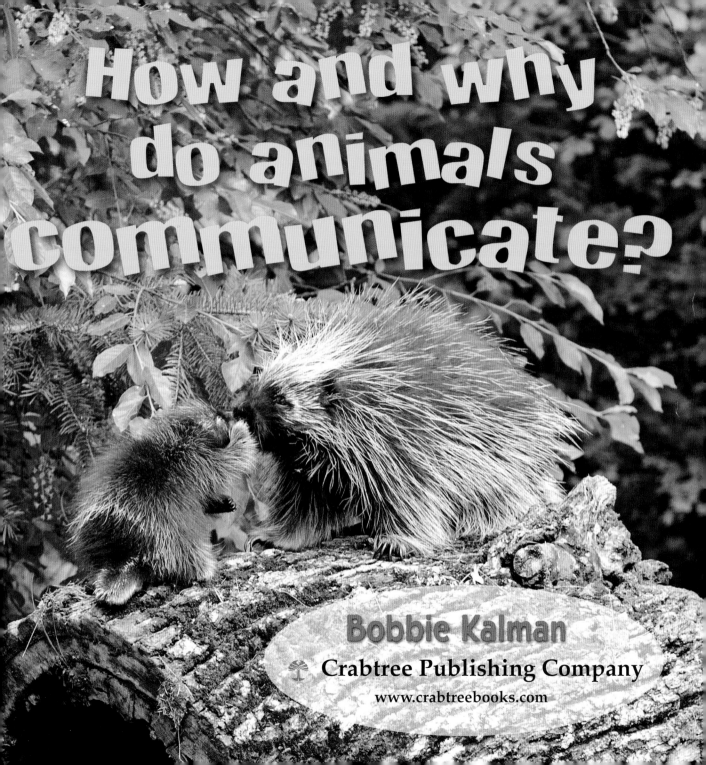

How and why do animals communicate?

Bobbie Kalman

Crabtree Publishing Company

www.crabtreebooks.com

All About Animals Close-Up

Dedicated by Samantha Crabtree
For Olivia Galvin
You are so beautiful and bright, you shine.
I love you dearly, Aunty Sam

Author and editor-in-chief
Bobbie Kalman

Publishing plan research and development
Reagan Miller

Editor
Kathy Middleton

Proofreader
Crystal Sikkens

Design
Bobbie Kalman
Katherine Berti
Samantha Crabtree (logo)

Photo research
Bobbie Kalman

Prepress technician
Samara Parent

Print and production coordinator
Margaret Amy Salter

Photographs and Illustrations
Thinkstock: page 17 (full page); page 20 (bottom);
   page 21 (bottom left and right)
Cover and all other photographs by Shutterstock

Library and Archives Canada Cataloguing in Publication

Kalman, Bobbie, author
    How and why do animals communicate? / Bobbie Kalman.

(All about animals close-up)
Includes index.
Issued in print and electronic formats.
ISBN 978-0-7787-1464-4 (bound).--ISBN 978-0-7787-1470-5 (pbk.).--
ISBN 978-1-4271-7636-3 (pdf).--ISBN 978-1-4271-7630-1 (html)

    1. Animal communication--Juvenile literature. I. Title.

QL776.K338 2015   j591.59   C2014-908184-7
                                          C2014-908185-5

Library of Congress Cataloging-in-Publication Data

Kalman, Bobbie.
    How and why do animals communicate? / Bobbie Kalman.
      pages cm. -- (All about animals close-up)
    Includes index.
    ISBN 978-0-7787-1464-4 (reinforced library binding : alk. paper) --
    ISBN 978-0-7787-1470-5 (pbk. : alk. paper) --
    ISBN 978-1-4271-7636-3 (electronic pdf : alk. paper) --
    ISBN 978-1-4271-7630-1 (electronic html : alk. paper)
    1. Animal communication--Juvenile literature. I. Title.

QL776.K338 2015
591.59--dc23
                                          2014049628

Crabtree Publishing Company

www.crabtreebooks.com   1-800-387-7650

Printed in Canada/042015/BF20150203

Published in Canada
Crabtree Publishing
616 Welland Ave.
St. Catharines, Ontario
L2M 5V6

Published in the United States
Crabtree Publishing
PMB 59051
350 Fifth Avenue, 59th Floor
New York, New York 10118

Published in the United Kingdom
Crabtree Publishing
Maritime House
Basin Road North, Hove
BN41 1WR

Published in Australia
Crabtree Publishing
3 Charles Street
Coburg North
VIC 3058

Contents

How do you communicate?

People **communicate** to exchange information, ideas, thoughts, news, and feelings with others. They communicate by talking, writing, and creating music and pictures. How do animals communicate? Do they use cell phones? Find out how and why animals exchange information with other animals and people.

Many people today use cell phones, tablets, and computers to text others or chat with them.

Body language

People also use body language to communicate. Body language includes smiles, frowns, and **gestures** made with the hands and other body parts. Animals also use body language. Find out how they do it!

What do you think?

What kind of body language are the kids on this page using to show that they are angry, ashamed, or confused?

How animals communicate

Animals communicate to attract **mates**, scare enemies, hunt **prey**, or show love. They cannot speak, but they do make sounds and use different body parts to send messages. Animals also use their senses of sight, smell, hearing, taste, and touch to send and receive messages.

This skunk uses scent, or smell, to keep other animals, and people, away.

Some animals communicate using special body parts (see pages 12–13). Male frigate birds puff out their red throat sacs to attract mates.

throat sac

Gorillas make loud growling sounds and beat their chests to scare other animals away.

This baby bonobo is using body language to communicate. What do you think it is saying?

What do you think?

The skunk, bird, bonobo, and gorilla are all communicating. What message is each one sending? Which animals are using body language?

Sound messages

Some animals make sounds to scare away enemies. Tigers and lions are big cats that make long, loud, roaring sounds. Smaller cats, such as cougars, cannot roar. They growl. What other sounds do animals make? How and why do they make these sounds?

Tigers make loud roaring sounds to scare away other animals. How do their teeth and ears also show their anger?

Cougars cannot roar, but their growls are still loud and scary. How is this cougar's face scary, too?

tiger

cougar

Elephants communicate using loud calls that they make by blowing air through their trunks. They also stomp their feet to make sounds that can be heard far away by other elephants.

Why do wolves howl? Find out on page 17.

Why do wolves howl? Find out on page 17.

What do you think?

What kinds of sounds do dogs, frogs, and birds make? What three sounds do you make? What does each of your sounds communicate?

Touch is communication

Many animals use touch to say hello or show love to other animals. Mothers often cuddle their babies to make them feel safe and warm. Animals also use touch to fight and hurt one another.

This fox mother is licking her kit, or baby, to show her love. Licking is like kissing.

This mother gorilla is hugging and kissing her baby.

Many monkeys, like this mother monkey, show their love by grooming, or cleaning, one another.

Grooming makes monkeys feel relaxed and helps them bond with other monkeys in their troop, or group.

Kangaroos fight to show other kangaroos that they are the boss. Which other animals fight to show that they are the strongest? (See page 17.)

(See page 17.)

What do you think?

How do people use touch to show how they feel? How do these children feel about one another?

I can look bigger!

Some animals have body parts that they can open or puff up to make themselves look bigger or scarier to **predators**. Some male animals use these body parts to make themselves more attractive to female animals.

This lizard has opened its neck frill, or flap, to scare away a predator.

dewlap

An anole's throat sac, called a dewlap, makes this lizard look much bigger.

vocal sac

Using its huge **vocal sac**, this male spring frog is calling for a mate.

When an owl butterfly is seen upside down, the patterns on its wings resemble the face of an owl. The butterfly appears much bigger than it really is.

Teaching and learning

Many bird and **mammal** parents teach their babies how to move, find food and water, and avoid predators. Teaching and learning are ways of communicating. Most animals teach by showing how to do something, such as climbing trees or hunting.

This black bear mother is teaching her cub how to climb a tree. Some babies fall and hurt themselves, so the mother stays close to the cub. Why is the cub on the right crying?

What do you think?

How do your parents and teachers teach you new information or skills that you need to learn? Name three tools you use for learning. Which is your favorite?

The oldest female elephant in a **herd** shows the young ones where to find water to drink.

This fox mother is showing her kits how to hunt and where to find food. Foxes hunt small animals, such as mice and rabbits. They also eat plants.

15

Group communication

Some animals, such as wolves and dolphins, live in big groups. They travel and hunt together. They keep in touch with their groups and warn one another of danger. They use sound and body language to communicate.

Dolphins travel in huge groups called pods or schools. They swim close together and communicate by using movements and sounds such as clicks, whistles, barks, and grunts. Each dolphin has its own sound, which is like its name. Dolphins recognize one another by their special sounds.

Wolves are part of groups called packs. They live and hunt together.

Wolves howl to let members of their pack know where they are.

They bare their teeth when they are angry. **Dominant** wolves show that they are in charge by holding other wolves beneath them. The weaker wolves must obey.

Singing and dancing

Some male animals perform songs and dances to attract females so they can mate, or make babies together. Many kinds of birds sing or perform these courtship dances.

The two gray herons above, and the blue-footed boobies below, are performing courtship dances.

This lark is singing to find a mate. It also sings to tell other birds to stay out of its **territory**.

Male humpback whales sing long songs made up of sounds like moans, chirps, roars, and snores. Each song lasts about fifteen minutes. No one is sure why they sing, but scientists think it may be to attract a mate or to help them navigate, or find their way, in the ocean.

Not only do humpbacks sing, they also put on a show to impress female whales. They breach, or leap high out of the water, to show how strong they are.

How are they the same?

The pictures on these pages show some similar body language used by animals and people. Match the pictures with the same body language or type of communication. Do you think the messages sent by the animals are the same as those sent by people? Why or why not?

②

①

Which ones match?

The matching pictures are 1 and 5; 2 and 4; 3 and 6. Did you get them all?

20

③

④

⑤

⑥

People and animals

Animals that live with or near people have learned to communicate to humans what they need or want. They use sounds, body language, or both. What and how are these animals communicating? How does your pet let you know what it wants? How do you get what you want?

Name three ways this girl is using body language to get what she wants.

Learning more

Books

Kalman, Bobbie. *How do animals communicate?* (Big Science Ideas).
Crabtree Publishing Company, 2009.

Kalman, Bobbie. *What senses do animals have?* (Big Science Ideas).
Crabtree Publishing Company, 2009.

Kalman, Bobbie. *Animal Mothers* (My World). Crabtree Publishing
Company, 2011.

Kaner, Etta. *Animal Talk: How Animals Communicate through Sight,
Sound and Smell* (Animal Behavior). Kids Can Press, 2002.

Websites

YouTube: Secrets of Animal Communication
www.youtube.com/watch?v=MXTezlwNyM4

NatureWorks: Communication
www.nhptv.org/natureworks/nwep3.htm

Fact Monster: Animal Communication
www.factmonster.com/ipka/A0768578.html

Words to know

communicate (kuh-MYOO-ni-keyt) verb
To pass along information using sounds,
senses, and body movements
dominant (DOM-uh-nuh-nt) adjective
Ruling or controlling
gesture (JES-cher) noun A hand or
body movement used to express a
thought or feeling
herd (hurd) noun A group of elephants
made up of female relatives and
their young
mammal (MAM-uh-l) noun A
warm-blooded animal that gives
birth to live young
mate (meyt) noun A partner for
making babies

predator (PRED-uh-tawr) noun An
animal that hunts other animals for food
prey (prey) noun An animal that is
hunted by another animal
territory (TER-i-tawr-ee) noun The
area that is claimed and defended by
an animal
vocal sac (VOH-kuh-l sak) noun
A large pouch of skin which frogs fill
with air to make sounds

A noun is a person, place, or thing.
A verb is an action word that tells you
what someone or something does.
An adjective is a word that tells you
what something is like.

Index